Street Sailing

By Matt Gilbert

Editor: Matthew M. C. Smith
Artist: Ben Pearce

www.blackboughpoetry.com
Twitter: @blackboughpoems
Insta: @blackboughpoetry
FB: BlackBoughpoetry

First published by Black Bough Poetry in 2023.
Copyright © 2023

LEGAL NOTICE

The right of Matthew M. C. Smith to be identified as the editor of this work has been asserted in accordance with the Copyright, Designs and Patents Act 1988. Matt Gilbert reserves the copyright to his work.
Typesetting by Matthew M. C. Smith. Artwork by Ben Pearce.

All rights reserved. No part of this book may be reproduced, stored in a retrieval system, or transmitted in any form, or by any means; electronic, mechanical, photocopying, without prior permission from the author and editor. However, short extracts may be quoted on social media. Matthew M. C. Smith has asserted his right under Section 77 of the Copyright, Designs and Patents Act 1988 to be identified as the editor of this work.

Cover illustration: Liverpool Street, by Ben Pearce.

About the Author:

Matt Gilbert is a freelance copywriter, who also writes a blog about place, books and other distractions at richlyevocative.net. He has had poems published in a wide variety of places, including: *Acumen*, *Atrium*, *Finished Creatures* and *The Storms*. He was Black Bough poetry's *Silver Branch* poet in September 2022. Twitter: @richlyevocative Insta: @richlyevocative richlyevocative.net

About the Artist:

Ben Pearce is an illustrator and animation director. He's worked on projects for a wide range of high-profile clients including Google, Facebook, BBC and TED to name a few. Ben recently worked as a director on "The Headspace Guide to Meditation", an animated TV series aired on Netflix. The series won a Daytime EMMY Award 2022 for Outstanding Main Title and Graphic Design. www.benpearce.com Insta: albionworks

About the Editor:

Matthew M. C. Smith is a poet-editor from Swansea, Wales. He studied for a PhD at the University of Wales, Swansea, on Robert Graves and Celticism. He runs *Black Bough Poetry*, *The Silver Branch project* and global poetry fest @TopTweetTuesday on Twitter. Matthew is the author of *The Keeper of Aeons*, *Origin: 21 Poems* and pamphlet 'Paviland: Ice and Fire'. Twitter: @MatthewMCSmith Insta: @smithmattpoet Also on FB.

There is something simultaneously powerful and unsettling about Gilbert's writing, as he cuts into the centre of a universal fear: what is it like to be seen – truly seen – and can we ever recover from this unmasking? Each poem haunts the page with precise imagery and a linguistic dexterity that illuminates the mammoth talent held in this book. Weaving between memory, present environments, and dreams of the future, this collection unpacks all the layers a man can hold and the depths a poet must go to uncover them. Gilbert is both man and poet: a tremendous addition to contemporary art and a courageous, sensitive embodiment of masculinity.

Briony Collins

Street Sailing is a collection that fizzes with the poet's powers of observation. Matt Gilbert is able to paint the seemingly everyday in a range of fresh and surprising colours. A grasshopper 'makes a myth of a whitewashed wall'; a crow arrives as 'a hole in bird form'; pavements become 'concrete seas'. Wherever Gilbert points us – whether the city, the coast or the countryside – there's warmth to be found, and a well-judged spoonful of whimsy. This is a collection to savour, from a skilled poet who encourages us to go out into the world with our eyes wide open.

Jen Feroze

It is a remarkable thing indeed to find a poet so in command of his craft so relatively early in his poetic journey. But so it is in the case of Matt Gilbert. This is a debut that feels too polished to be a poet's first outing: the deftest ringmastering of a circus of words, the keenest direction of a broad cast of characters, themes and ideas. By the end, you will wonder (as I did) just how Matt plans to engage and entertain us with whatever second act he must surely be at work on.

Mark Antony Owen

Each poem in this outstanding collection exists in its own right: snapshots of moments, objects and emotions all skillfully captured and framed by metaphor, imagery and form. Gilbert uses his distinctive voice to explore the uneasy co-existence of the urban and rural, the past and present, humans and animals. He has a true poet's eye for detail. The blurring of reality and imagination transform everyday occurrences into a fascinating and sometimes threatening landscape where the mystical and the urbane meet. These poems are alive: they have a heart-beat.

Kitty Donnelly

Editor's introduction

It's a real privilege to have worked on *Street Sailing*, a collection of poetry that has an invigorating, quirky and inventive feel, a book that gets into, and under, the fabric of society and the urban and natural environment.

Matt Gilbert's writing marvels in the spirit of place; his poetry wanders, camera-like, along overgrown tracks through woods, riverbanks and wastegrounds that are rewilding; he takes us on journeys to greening edgelands that spill into urban decay. Gilbert's eye pans, then zooms in, on the minutiae that most of us ignore, the neglected details of our physical environment. He is a descriptive, modern poet of nature with a scalpel-like pen and eye for the arresting image as he quietly transcribes, always searching for the near-perfect word and phrase. He plunges us into deep time, recording mysterious odysseys into the places, traces and symbols of the ancient past.

This is a poet who can write about anything and do so with a fresh take. Enjoy *Street Sailing* and shout out about it!

Matthew M. C. Smith, April 2023.

For Mum & Dad – I got there in the end!

Acknowledgements

Thank you to the following magazines, journals and e-journals, for first publishing versions of some of these poems: *Anthropocene* - 'How to Flatten the Moon', *Atrium* - 'Tickenham Hill' & 'Flower of Bristol', *Authora Australis* - 'Take the Second Exit' & 'Drowning Under Flowers', *Dawntreader (Indigo Dreams Publishing)* - 'Foxed', *Fevers of the Mind* - 'Ridley Road', Flights - 'Spalted Wood', *Green Ink* - 'Some Men and a Horse', *Ink Sweat & Tears* - 'Afoot', *Lothlorien Poetry Journal* - 'Beyond DIY', *Marble* - 'Domestic'.

Versions of some of the poems included appeared in *Black Bough Poetry's* own TopTweetTuesday, which has been invaluable for both discovering poetic peers and building an audience of my own.

Thanks to Matthew M. C. Smith, editor and fizzing ball of energy. Your encouragement, drive and passion has helped me imagine that I can, perhaps, start to call myself a poet.

Thanks to Nathalie for attentive listening.

Thanks to Sam, Leo & Abi for believing.

CONTENTS

Awake

Awake	2
Spalted wood	3
Grasshopper	4
Beyond DIY	5
Domestic	6
Some men and a horse	7
Urban rewilding	8
Landmarking	9
How to flatten the moon	10
Take the second exit	11
Drowning under flowers	12
Foxed	13

Afoot

Only Crow	16
A Dangling	17
Afoot	18
Rats, Upper Vatch Mill	19
Undercliff	20
Pebbles on the shore	21
Canalside nocturne	22
Bristle	23
Flower of Bristol	24
Tickenham Hill	25
At Black Nore Lighthouse	26
Seven Sisters	27

Acceptance

I made a mess of my own pathetic fallacy	30
A hammering	31
Street sailing	32
South London Satori	33
Garden bag resurrection	34
Goldfinched	35
A terror of twee trees	36
The nature present	37
Father's Day	38
Ridley Road	39
Forked	40
Aurochs	41
Recommended Reading	42
More Poetry	43

I

Awake

Awake

Desolation banshees out
and through the house,
memory sent scrambling
for her trousers:
What - the hell - was that?

Panicked synapses fumble
for a trace, at last recalling,
with a frazzled smile,
nothing but a fox,
turning the city inside out.

Spalted wood

Had to take it, didn't I? Have it,
remove that slice of tree heart,
revealed when clearing space for light
in the woods, blood-red stripe shining
through the middle, wordless seaside rock.

Strange to find such beauty, born of fighting
fungi, *ascomycetes,* or unsexed *imperfecti*,
dyeing the insides with lines of pigment,
expanding as they battle over territory,
unseen, until the tree dies, or is cut open.

Back at the house I flashed my trophy,
earning praise for craft I'd had no part in,
shelved my wooden lump, leaving it to sit
unvarnished, as the bright colour faded,
dulled to pink, until almost unremarkable.

Grasshopper

You made a myth of a whitewashed wall,
jarring ambassador in green,
casting, somehow, the house as stranger

As though it had attached itself to you,
transported to a pre-suburban state
where under carpet grass hills still roll.

Unsettled by your vital stillness,
we thought it time you were replaced,
outside, outsize presence too much to bear.

That ovipositor of yours should twitch,
life-wired, upcurving, stretching out,
we know what's best for you.

So quivering through the door,
I gave you back to the outside,
returned to find my world had shrunk.

Beyond DIY

Winter haunts the bathroom wall,
inviting damp to fill cold corners,
shape faceless negatives in mould.

Observed through steam when lying
in hot water, old discontents, reborn
as stains, small guilts on warping paint.

Faint apparitions of anxiety, surfacing
behind the taps, a recalled cast
of past mistakes, sketchy forms in white.

The angler-fish, all teeth and razor
patience, the eyeless soldier, broken flag,
the crooked bird, on unhinged wings.

Ghosts, condensed in two dimensions,
uneasy blot and patch, one day to be
exorcised, with new brushes, dipped in gloss.

Domestic

What we had once, shifted, became displaced
in black mould peppering cold corners of the house.

Pushed deep inside the boiler to come coughing
back, terse notes sent rattling up through buried pipes.

Feelings flaked under fine cracks on concrete gutter,
leaking back inside with rain, gaining access via windows.

Old senses hung slack within hinges, creaking boards,
tired paint, leering sofa stains, fabric worn by leaping boys.

Hope moved towards the bottom of the laundry basket,
nestling with out-of-favour leggings, once treasured t-shirts.

And our lost futures keep on rising, bursting back from photos
no longer facing, as we scan the dark from beds stair-flights apart.

Some men and a horse

There were ten of them, or so, stood around a horse,
all capped and slouched, except the boys kneeling
at the front, some of these great uncles, turned away,
unfocused, as older men stared down the barrel of a lens.

The sense I ought to feel, stronger than actual feeling,
as I look back into those reluctant photographic faces,
lips clamping woodbines, jug-eared and hard, in rumpled shirts,
related, somehow, to me, all distance there in black-and-white.

Heard later, that my great-grandfather fell from a horse,
dying on a different day, changing the view, if not the image,
forcing great-grandmother to leave, to go in search of work,
her departure a reminder, that cameras are not the same as mirrors.

Urban rewilding

Those woods on the ridge, through the window, if watched
from a certain angle, will roll over the roads, untame the suburbs,
reclaim the shape of old maps –

all chimneys and aerials can be bundled away, with a half-hunched flick
of the head, church spire and estate put out of sight, sent to the back
of the mullion, by the turn of your face.

Before every storey of the block to the east, is pushed from the frame,
the people swept off their feet, so that all city crows, the pigeons, the starlings
can safely be recast as rural, in a tidy green scene that never existed,

not like this, not like this.

Landmarking

They became the place
those towered hyper eyes,
charging cold white stone
with hot charisma, there
beneath a broken clock,
church reconsecrated
feral cathedral,
peregrine scrape on
South London cliff,
lording over prey below.

How to flatten the moon

Don't look, glance,
bring a glass,
not a Claude Glass,
though, do turn your back
as the guide suggests,
or, rather, turn your eye,
your heart away, ignoring
that fluttered nervy sensation
behind your ribs,
it's nothing
but a tired impulse
triggered the second
you approached
the bus stop,
saw hanging there
above the shelter's
upturned L
the rounded milky glint
of our almost full fat
satellite, stirrer of waves,
provider of rocky perspective,
of intimately distant reassurance,
to any who care to lift a chin,
at least since we first
dropped down from trees,
there it is, there it is,
all 7.342×10^{22} kg of it,
now ease the phone
from your pocket, point it up
towards our ancient friend,
then click.

Now you've done it.

Take the second exit

An Icarus with a witness
almost fell today,
caught itself instead

above a roundabout.
Bottom of the street,
around fourteen storeys

up – had there been a building
in that space, not air – filled
with rasping corvids. Jabbing

at a lone indignant rival,
sparrowhawk, reduced
to scrapping over hazy sky.

Very nearly overwhelmed,
but no one really noticed.
Rush hour cars kept coming,

oblivious to all but road.
Red and black, silver, blue,
relentless, petrol-powered

roulette balls, spinning on
through space. Drivers lurching
into gaps, desperate for their exit.

Drowning under flowers

There's an orange lifebuoy in the corner
of a field, a twenty-minute walk from
where I live, down a lane beside a station.

A green corridor of sorts, lined with ash
saplings and bramble, worn-wire, wind tossed
shreds of once-used plastic and wrinkled cans.

Eventually this sputters out, expelling foot passengers
onto the track that is the south circular at Dulwich.
Cross this, between impatient 4x4s, go into the park.

Belair, once a private estate – head north, almost
to the fence and there, sometimes, in high summer,
you'll see the strangest thing, this lifebuoy on a board.

Perched at the lip of a lake of rampant vegetation,
as if placed to save people coming here to drown
in wild flowers, lose themselves beneath the bedstraw.

Overcome at last by poppies and the vetch.
A suburban mythic, eerie conceit, half-attractive,
half-repulsive and near impossible to picture

come November. When this grey ditch is pooled
with water, remains picked over by tetchy, stick-leg
crows, once yet another year has passed.

Foxed

It must have cracked her body
like a nut, that train.

I doubt they stopped to look –
they never cleared her from the track.

Red fur, flattened body like a bog-man,
preserved unburied, because 'she is not one of us'.

You could see that from the final snarl,
all anguish-anger-shock ground-in.

Rictus grin stamped deeper into steel,
a short story of time-tabled further violence.

One furtive, final crossing bodily curtailed,
full-stopped and slammed towards the ballast.

Right there, for days on platform's end,
I couldn't not keep looking.

Especially when I saw the cub,
who'd made it to the other side.

Past a thin wire fence but that far only,
ending a tail-tangled death pile in dandelion.

In the absence of a ritual, a song of storied life,
I shall mark your empty legend.

II

Afoot

Only crow

Horror arrives
as a hole in bird form,
a ripple, a warp

in want of definition.
An absence in near space,
a blot to fill the air above

with doubt. It is a negative
angel, siren, ink-spot fiend,
shadow question mark.

Clearly not of ordinary
sky, this thing is
magnificence

on wings, until
a rust voice insists
otherwise:

I am crow, only crow.

A dangling

At first it was a single button,
arriving on its own, formed
in the air between two oaks

like an interned autumn leaf,
found hanging in October,
suspended from unseen webs.

Except there was no web, no thread
– as if it just belonged, the button
stayed, floating for no reason

until the cuff began to form,
sprouting from that plastic seed,
a rootless, hovered piece of cloth.

Eventually, a sleeve, arms empty,
followed by pocket, collar, yoke,
a placket, right front, then left

bottom hem, back body part, a plain
white shirt, emerging without context,
in the middle of the local woods.

Miracle in cotton, shockingly mundane,
– I have no urge to touch the thing,
cannot fathom why it came.

Afoot

Only, when your face slams
into solid glass, somewhere outside
Dorking – a squared-off edge

unmentioned in map or guide –
do you realise what's going on.
Presence noted by a watchful

deer, wary at the edge of woods,
the skulk of abandoned pill boxes,
where yews suck on dirty chalk.

At last, the scene makes sense;
you've strayed inside a postcard,
having used up all your stamps.

Rats, Upper Vatch Mill

From here, I still see sets of eyes reflecting
darkness, snouts and rope pink tails trailing
out, layered in between sticks and crumpled
paper, like rat lasagne.

But memory plays tricks. That's not quite how
it went – all bodies had been neatly tucked
inside the pile, ready to make a bonfire of any
creature who'd dared stray among the chickens

and lost their wits enough to take the poison, which
would send them twitching into unexpected death.
I was not the executioner, although I lit the match,
watched flames lick, consume late-summer's debris.

Of all the things to recall about a garden:
Ian's roses, haunted mill-pond, twisted apple trees,
awkwardly sloped lawns, I dwell on burning rats.

Undercliff

Called here by a book, I slip in on a foot-worn
path, familiar from pages turned over long ago.
The way soon roughens, jagging up and down

within the woods, thick today with summer
green, rain-slick below worn crags, teetered
here, on the edge of prehistoric coast.

Fern fronds unfurl in every gap, between
landslip craters, full with stewy, tea-brown
water, air alive with birdcalls, measured out

through density, not volume. Cries rising
up among tall living trees, marching on,
between cut piles of dead,

die-back-stricken ash – and at the heart,
anchored on the shore side of the track,
an old oak, tailored in a suit of epiphytes.

Thick limbs fur-soft with moss and brake,
life multiplied by life. Staggered by its presence
I have to stop. Together briefly, we are a pair

of pilgrims, passing on the road. We touch
 – cold hand, rough bark. To note I saw this
could never be enough, I have to say, we met.

Pebbles on the shore

Heads bent, eyes skim the shingle,
sorting through tide scatterings:
rainbowed, ovoid lumps, jagged shards,
worn brick and glass. We are helpless then,

before the wet wink of the imagined prize,
radiant as it summons us to stoop and pick
and palm our own unique, elusive beauty,
hidden from every other seeker.

A slick fragment of time, slipped amongst
junked chunks of sea-grey aggregate and grit.
And for all we may suspect this notion
is flawed – stopping in one place, in fact,

to sift, would be more productive – who
can truly resist supposing that when we pass,
walking shaky lines, our fated rock will be there,
lying on the beach, waiting for this moment?

Canalside nocturne

Silver blue at night, they sleep beneath
not quite static water; alongside the solid
of the towpath. Those glass-eyed blocks

of flats and former warehouses –
squat-square-silent: the rippled liquid
bodies of a city in reverse.

Projected in-between bike bones,
drowned supermarket trolleys and
suspect, over-weighty cases, strangled

in the weeds, at dawn. They reassemble,
fainter in the light, hard-by hissing
goose gangs and nervous moorhens,

take their daytime form, as rectangular
reflections snagged within the old canal;
side-entrance to a shimmer, shadow world.

Bristle

Light jabs of rain arrive against my face,
like firm strokes from a metal pinhead hairbrush,
poking me back in, on foot from Temple Meads,
along a stretch of Avon. Today, wind-shredded,
the river shrugs, surging toffee brown towards the centre,
as discordant gull hoards scream: *'Not you again'* –
cries shattering on contact with air and in their midst,
one great black-backed fiend, carts a headless pigeon off
to finish on the dirty water, while nearby, reflex shoppers
shuffle round the concrete remains of Broadmead,
'Well, what did you expect?' ask rattled chimney pots,
smokeless, scowling, chess piece kings, throned on worn
Victorian rooftops, sharp crenelated crowns low slung,
above the gloomy faces of rambling relic buildings,
shaded, in the city's signature pennant stone, 4B pencil grey.
I'm back to visit, between storms with names and it seems
we've changed, my hometown and me.

Flower of Bristol

At 16 I used to carry flowers home for Mum, from Dave
the florist, at the bottom of St Michael's Hill, a sharp
rising urban mountain, all grind and vicious angle.

A bastard all the way, to where gallows once threw shade,
tar-coated dead swinging at the top. I'd trudge up there,
embarrassed by my package, screaming out in pink

and orange, passing Special K's, 'St Michael's on the Mount
Without', oblivious to The Robin Hood, The Royal Infirmary,
The Slave Trader's Arms, Slave Trader's Alms Houses.

Blissfully unaware of all the places proudly named for Colston,
Edward, our celebrated local son. Benefactor of the chosen few,
wealth accumulated off-stage in blood, out on the Atlantic,

or infernal fields, far across its western edge. Half a million
lives despatched on Bristol ships alone, unmarked unless on
cargo manifests, no edifice, or pubs for them. Disregarded

decade after decade, until that statue took a dip, down
in the harbour, a reckoning, some denounced as a step too far.
As though a city's dirty past should stay unwashed for good.

Tickenham Hill

Somewhere beneath that listening ridge
the winds are gossiping again, in tongues
beyond the most vague and coarse translation.

A breezy sonic-catalogue of air let loose,
wheezes in, behind walkers staggering up
the slopes, outroaring the M5 at every step.

Until the top, with banks now bare again,
fit for prehistoric sentries to cast their eyes
across the stretching flats. Land Yeo wriggling

off towards the estuary's greyed-out islands.
Wales industrious over fast brown waves,
not quite yet the sea, still almost as strange.

It is a chafing edge of sorts, rabbits racing
over grass towards the woods. Not waiting
to witness other beings cloud over the horizon.

At Black Nore Lighthouse

Lofted above a scaggy, driftwood scattered beach,
lording over chunks of rock, a stilted steam-punk
iron torch, painted in off-white. All warnings retired

and snubbed by squatting seabirds – resting up
on tiny Ynys Deny/Denny Island, out amongst
the sandbanks – in cackling mockery of borders.

Behind us, a small town rapidly expands.
Ahead, the waters of the Severn unite the coast
of post-industrial South Wales with this western edge

of England. Here, someone's left a fire to smoulder,
its acrid smoke ghosts drift across the channel,
where silhouettes of distant hills loom, like invitations.

Seven Sisters

Abrupt above white cliffs it hangs, blood
echo of every ancient creature suspended
here, at the crumbling end of England.

Over grassed chalk, wings stop all air,
statue head a searchlight, flashing, willing
prey to come slipping blithely into view.

A kestrel star – stage set by a billion fallen
foraminifera, all consciousness now rock,
sixty metres higher than the shore.

Purpose fixed, indifferent to gawping booted
witnesses, eyes held up for ceaseless seconds,
petrified beneath such hovering perfection.

And then it drops - that feathered drone -
obliging gravity to meet its needs, talons open,
time let slip once more, before a restive sea.

III

Acceptance

I made a mess of my own pathetic fallacy

Lyme Regis let me down when I went there
to insert myself into a meta fiction – make
a memory from the memory of a book.

'The French Lieutenant's Woman.' Not for
its romance, Smithson was too stiff, Sarah
Woodruff more Victorian wet dream

than living woman. At least, that's what
I felt when I read it at 16. As if I'd had a clue.
What I did like was the Undercliff, the way

it was described, birthing a place far thicker
than the paper it appeared on. And why, years
later, when my marriage fell apart, I stood there

on the cobb, at the spot where a woman who
had never been, faced out to sea. Black hooded,
waiting like a ghost. My old blue anorak would

have to do instead, as I asked an urgent question
of the waves, which were not behaving as I wanted
– not fierce, or dark enough. And all the other tourists'

chatter forced me to shout inside my head: What happens
when the storm of love subsides? Where should we put
the past? I got no easy answers, the bay speaks only water

and made my trousers slightly damp. Yes, salt foam went
flying, but wasn't spitting for my grief. A few gulls cried
out in passing, wheeling overhead – not, I think, for me.

A hammering

The three of us are strangers,
though we all share ears and eyes,
trained now on an abstract scrawl
of branches, searching out the source

of the drum that drew us, heads tilted,
necks craned. We converse in awkward
grins, exchanged as we're each gifted
a piece of punctuated silence,

becoming briefly lost to the rattling fact
of beak on trunk. As a woodpecker fulfils
its mission, unconscious that long miles
east, the thumping stems from missiles.

No one mentions over-crowded trains,
or basements, mines, refugees, a war,
all unwilling to break the spell, the comfort
found, in a small bird's insistent hammer.

Street sailing

This morning the houses are brick-built
boats, windows flashing hope as light
back into the sky, tower blocks moored
liners, pavements concrete seas,
pedestrians, shoe-sailors, plotting
routes to circumvent the doldrums,
courses set for the islands of possibility,
somewhere out there, beyond the break of day.

Come evening, urban mariners return,
streets harbour bulky cargoes,
pallets laden down with stress, disquiet,
frustration – anxious to be unloaded
with the tide, stowed behind thick
wooden doors, or beachcombed cardboard
covers, tied-up and closed against the night,
before tomorrow's voyages must be underway.

South London Satori

Perhaps there was a hint of it in the slinking moon,
peering out from gaps among fast scudding clouds

the previous night, as evening's granite mist-hounds
hunted down stray patches of empty winter sky.

Ahead of revelation in the morning, when in a moment
on an icy pavement at one end of Railton Road –

next to a crazy jumble-pile of bikes, wedged in between
bay-window and a wall, alongside a scrawled sign in red

offering up repairs, the sun squeezed through a hole
within the tightly-terraced row. Cut through biting air

with a dazzling knife of light, exactly at the time a crocodile
of school kids came singing down the street, outraging

a sparrow quarrel, busy shouting in a hedge. So they took
flight right beneath my eyes, ambushed my face into a smile.

Utterly unexpected, as I was walking home, before my thoughts
raced back, to rue the cold continued absence of a bus.

Garden bag resurrection

A crumpled, green face sags
beneath the hedge, revealing age lines
born of foliage. The clipped, dry, stalk
death-mask of unwanted matter –
except for a poke of desiccated cuttings,
where worker bees navigate a narrow gap;
one, two, three, they make their way inside,
reinventing space, bridging hope and ruin,
as each returns to greet a buried queen.

Goldfinched

A feathered lump of life, arriving,
changed the street within five steps,
song bubbling out like smoke from
the rim of a long-cool chimney.

At distance, the small shape seemed
entirely made of sound and blurry
silhouette, so I filled out its form
from memory, painting in red cheeks,

dabbing on some golden flecks,
preparing wings to shine, contrast
with darker tips and primaries –
a charm all by itself.

A terror of twee trees

There's a row of hornbeams
on a road nearby that look to me
like dancers, bodies ripped and

fleshy. Wood-hard muscles tensed
as if each figure has been frozen,
midway through whip-wild twists

of ecstasy, soundtracked by the sap
silent music of its own life force.
I think this, even though I doubt

I should impart human form to trees,
fearing something cheap about the notion.
Never cool, this sort of sentimental gush,

so, I must stress, these lives are plants,
around them, shit and litter – cars, racing
for a roundabout, their drivers never give

a second glance to these suburban trunks.
That said, I cannot help myself, I still
find something moving in the scene.

The Nature Present

For months it is a drunken Y,
twisting, not quite steady
on its planted feet.

A cussed presence, dark
spiked and gnarly, softened
only by the fuzzed patina

of the lichen on its branches.
Knots and wrinkles, worn heavy,
some distance from the whiplash

elastic shoots of youth – but then,
like an aching clubber, is drawn back,
irresistibly, to the dancefloor,

by the honey-hook of a pulsing
May. The sort of tune old limbs
do not easily forget.

Suddenly it's spring, thick, green
again and to prove the sap still rises,
the tree drops all the classic moves,

revealing blossom scarlet-pink
enough to make a fuchsia blush.
And a young boy, not much moved

by plants, is stirred, recalls for this
one birthday month: that's a hawthorn,
my nature present's back.

Father's day

That the tall plant drawing bees ahead of us
is verbena. That the fragrant claw-like twist
of tree you are about to climb – magnolia,
means less to you than the fact that I,
for once, remembered, to bring a snack,

is a truth acknowledged with a small round
of shoulder, briefly pressed to mine.
And for the time it takes the sun to warm
our forearms, before it's draped once more
by cloud, my dad-stripes are assured.

Ridley Road

Saturday shoppers all spoke hard cash,
crinkling blue notes from frantic hand to hand,
for translation into the languages of bread;
luggage, mirrors, bedsheets, ackee, saltfish, oranges.

CDs piled high, crackling out of speakers hoping
to sell themselves, catch ears by jangling chords
like sonic change. *Sweet Mother* bursting out
from under cover, sailing over stalls,

before snagging on soft piles of towels, fading
cadences lingering near friends eyeing sweet
potatoes, lips pursed. Assessing apples, plums,
or chickens swinging from yellow metal stalls

like gibbets, butcher's eyes intent on plucking
potential clients – not considering how market days
once started between Victorian policemen's teeth,
as whistles. Turning market into match day scramble.

The old shrill signal echoes now in wrinkled faces,
weighing fruit in punch-bowl palms, testing pears
for ripe and heft, attending to subtle bruisings
of banana, re-imagining that taste, first met

years before, holding out unspoken hope,
appealing for another chance, to feel the fruit give,
as berry sugar softness yields to mouth and tooth
and tongue, back home, or on the way.

Forked

Early May, they're back, like kids
grabbing at your face to get attention.
Yanking chins skyward, with joyful screams,
four, five, six, circling the eaves of a street

corner house. Poking at a blocked-up
memory of nest, before the party's off,
hurtling around other rooftops, further
down the street. Forcing my mouth to fold,

mirror the crescent of their wings,
smile up a familiar shape, recalled in Irish,
as gabhlán gaoithe – the *forked one of the wind*

– their presence a guilty gift. Until, when
autumn drops, they're gone and as
with all the years before, I'm bereft, then
left to wonder if we'll see their like again.

Aurochs

Behind glass it might be
sculpted, the backlit borrowed
skull throws sharp curved shadow
over ages, forehead retaining
the stone axe-head, once
smashed, with fear-fuelled force,

between its eyes,
by a someone, unaware
this undoing act would
stick there for millennia,
a fragment of the weapon
crack-lodged, as if grown –

shh,

listen, this colossal bone-lump
sings, essence bursting
to slip the case, set horned gods
twitching, as reskinned
it runs, back out into the open,

hooves rising,
        pound a fatal drum,
wind whistles,
        nostrils flare,
        blood fires,
prehistoric beast,

awake!

RECOMMENDED READING

Check out these titles from the Bough and friends:

The Black Bough Poetry Library
(all titles available on Amazon)

Deep Time Vol 1 (Black Bough, 2020)
Deep Time Vol 2 (Black Bough, 2020)
Christmas & Winter Vol 1 (Black Bough, 2020)
Christmas & Winter Vol 2 (Black Bough, 2021)
Dark Confessions (Black Bough, 2021)
Freedom-Rapture (Black Bough, 2021)
Under Photon Crowns – Dai Fry (Black Bough, 2021)
Nights on the Line – individual collection by M.S. Evans (Black Bough 2022)
Sun-Tipped Pillars Of Our Hearts (Black Bough, 2022)
Christmas & Winter Vol 3 (Black Bough 2022)
Afterfeather (Black Bough, 2022)
Duet of Ghosts (Black Bough, 2022)
Sound and Vision (online only, 2023)

Publications by Matthew M. C. Smith:

Origins: 21 Poems – Matthew M C Smith (Amazon, 2018)
The Keeper of Aeons – Matthew M C Smith (Broken Spine, 2022)
Pamphlet - Paviland: Ice and Fire (Black Bough Poetry) 2023

Forthcoming Titles

Tutankhamun Centenary Anthology (Black Bough 2023)
The Wasteland Centenary Anthology (Black Bough 2023)

MORE POETRY

We love to boost poets across the world. Here are some recommended poetry books/ anthologies.

The Water Engine, Ankh Spice, Femme Salvé Books (2021)

Waterbearer, Stuart McPherson, Broken Sleep Books (2022).

River Ghosts, Merril D. Smith, Nightingale and Sparrow (2022).

Nightjars, Z.R. Ghani and Andy MacGregor (2022).

The Crow Gods, Sarah Connor, Sídhe Press (2023).

The Birds, The Rabbits, The Trees, Briony Collins, Broken Sleep Books (2023).

The Mask, Eli Horan, The Broken Spine (2021) – book of the month on the Black Bough website, March 2023.

The Dredging of Rituals, Louise Mather (2022) – book of the month on the Black Bough website, September 2022.

Against the Woods' Dark Trunks, Jack B. Bedell, Mercer University Press (2022).

The Colour of Hope, Jen Feroze, Matador Press (2020).

In Dangerous Hours, Kitty Donnelly, Indigo Dreams (2022).

Moon Jellyfish Can Barely Swim, Ness Owen, Parthian Books (2023).

Panic Response, John McCullough, Penned in the Margins (2022).

The Storms Anthologies – check out a dazzling array of poems from Ireland and the rest of the world, edited by Damien B. Donnelly and guest editors.

Bold Magazine: an anthology on Masculinities. The Broken Spine (2023).

Poetry Wales – make sure you consider taking out a membership to this iconic magazine.

Nights on the Line

M. S. Evans

MATTHEW M.C. SMITH
The Keeper of Aeons

THE BROKEN SPINE

Printed in Poland
by Amazon Fulfillment
Poland Sp. z o.o., Wrocław